TV COUNTRY FAVOURITES

From the BBC and Yorkshire TV

HILARY GRAY

Published by Atlantic Publishers, Holebottom Farm, Hebden,
Skipton, North Yorkshire, BD23 5DL.

ISBN: 0 906899 92 3

First published 1998

Contains material distributed under licence from
BBC Worldwide Limited

Selected images:
© The BBC and BBC Worldwide Limited 1998,
by arrangement with BBC Worldwide Limited
(Cover & photographs on pages 47, 48, 50, 51, 52, 55, 59, 62, 63,
66, 70, 72, 74, 76, 78, 79, 80, 84, 85, 87, 89, 91, 94)

© Yorkshire Television Ltd.
(Cover & photographs on pages 5, 6, 8, 9, 10, 11, 12, 13, 14, 15,
19, 20, 22, 23, 24, 25, 26(lower), 27, 28, 30, 32, 33, 35, 37(left),
38, 40, 41, 42(lower), 43, 44)

Design and layout: Trevor Ridley
Printed by The Amadeus Press Ltd, Huddersfield, West Yorkshire

British Cataloguing in Publication Data
A catalogue record for this book is available from the British Library

CONTENTS

INTRODUCTION

It's no happy accident that many of our favourite and most enduring television programmes are set in country locations. *Last of the Summer Wine* last year celebrated its 25th anniversary, making it the longest running sitcom in the world. *Emmerdale*, too, notched up its 25th year and is still going from strength to strength. *Heartbeat* with its gentle nostalgia is shown in 36 countries and continues to enjoy viewing figures of 18 million per episode.

Ballykissangel, a relative newcomer, has put Avoca, County Wicklow, firmly on the map and although *Hamish Macbeth*, *All Creatures Great and Small* and *The Darling Buds of May* are no longer on our screens, tourists still flock to the respective locations to see the countryside which brought the stories alive.

So what has made these series so popular? Perhaps viewers are intrigued by the idea of a country community where everyone knows everyone else and anything is likely to happen - and very often does! Or do these programmes appeal to the seasoned couch potatoes who like the idea of visiting the countryside but prefer to do so simply by turning on the telly and staying in the comfort of their favourite armchair?

Here we take a look at seven popular series which, between them, have kept over 101.7 MILLION viewers glued to their screens. We hear about how the programmes came into being, listen to a bit of gossip from behind the scenes and celebrate the secrets of their success.

1
EMMERDALE

The first episode of *Emmerdale Farm* was transmitted on 16th October, 1972. Donald Bavistock, then director of programmes at Yorkshire Television, had asked former actor and stage playwright Kevin Laffan to create a farming soap.

Explains Keith Richardson, Controller of Drama for Yorkshire Tyne Tees Television, 'The idea was to do a television version of *The Archers*. When it first went on air it went out as a lunchtime show. It was only going to be 26 episodes but the response was such that we were commissioned to do more and it moved round the schedule from lunchtime to an evening show twice a week. From January 1st,

1997, it moved to three.'

Initially, the small country village of Arncliffe was chosen to represent the fictional village of

The Woolpack - Beckindale's famous watering-hole

Home Farm, Emmerdale

Beckindale. 'In fact, we probably chose the wrong place because it was actually rather far away from base. As it was only for 26 weeks, we would film in the village for a number of episodes and then go back and shoot the studio stuff. When we got permission to carry on with the show, it became too expensive to constantly take a unit up there. We had to have overnight stays in hotels, so we looked around and we found further locations nearer to the Leeds studios.'

The interiors of the houses, pubs and cafes we saw on screen were a mixture of real location and studio sets. Last year, the *Emmerdale* studios moved from a converted ex-woollen mill in Farsley to a location near the main studios in Kirkstall, Leeds. The new location is reputed to be the largest television studio in the

world. Dedicated entirely to *Emmerdale* sets, it was opened by John Major on 6th January, 1997. The transition had taken three weeks and involved moving and rebuilding fifteen sets from the previous production centre, including a fully working pub and post office, complete with fully operational lottery machine. There are also three fully fitted kitchens in the studio.

The programme was originally publicised as 'the living story of the Sugden family – the excitement of country life around' – but as viewing tastes changed, it was felt that although they had a loyal audience who had been with them since the outset, the programme was failing to attract a younger audience whose misguided

Panoramic views in *Emmerdale* country are amongst the most spectacular in the UK (LEEDS CITY COUNCIL)

Amiable landlord Alan Turner (Richard Thorp) and Jo (Julie Peasgood) give gossip Betty plenty to talk about

perception was that the programme was all about farming .

Says Keith Richardson, 'We dropped the word 'Farm' in 1989. We felt we needed to expand the programme to allow younger characters in. It wasn't any longer rooted around the one farm, it was really a community. We then introduced younger characters and while this did alienate some of the older audience, who wanted it to remain exactly as it was, I think in most instances, they stayed with us but we had attracted a younger audience as well.'

Over the years there have been well over a

hundred writers and in recent times, plenty of racy storylines, not least amongst the younger cast members, keeping the viewing figures at a buoyant 11-12 million for each of the three weekly episodes. One of the *Emmerdale* younger set is Rebecca Loudonsack who was sixteen when she joined the cast as Emma Cairns.

She recalls, 'I was originally called Poppy and they told me at the third audition that Poppy was a bit mysterious and that she had a secret. I wondered what that could be, then next day when I came home, dad said he'd had a phone

Frank Tate (Norman Bowler) and Rachel Hughes (Glenda McKay) at Kim Tate's 'grave'. Kim was later to shock Frank - and *Emmerdale* viewers - by making a dramatic 'come-back' from the dead.

Dingles' new bus service – Marlon (Mark Charnock) and Albert (Bobby Knutt) try to attract Betty Eagleton's custom (Paula Tilbrook)

call and he believed I was playing a thirteen-year-old who was pregnant! I thought 'Wow! What more could I ask for? My first part on television and it's a good one!'

Paul Fox, who plays Will, Emma's screen brother, had a dramatic storyline last year when Will was held hostage by a nubile young kidnapper. He remembers these scenes with mixed feelings... 'It was fun but really hard as well. I spent quite a few days just tied up in this disused barn in the middle of nowhere. That was quite tough but I got on really well with Polly who played Fiona (the kidnapper). We had a great laugh.'

At some points, the action got pretty violent so just how realistic was it? Paul laughs, 'You

sometimes see things on telly and it doesn't look too good when they're trying to stage it so, on the take, I just said to Polly, "Go for it, give me a good slap!" and she certainly did!'

Sparks also flew when Kelly Windsor had a torrid affair with her schoolteacher, Tom, but on set, things were decidedly frosty! Adele, who plays Kelly, confesses that their scenes weren't always as romantic as they looked...

'We had a right laugh but we had to film in this dingy old bedsit place and it was freezing! Every scene that me and Jed did (Jeremy Turner-Welch who played Tom) was always in the cold.

'In one scene, just before Christmas, it was really sub-zero. It was supposed to be all sexy and Kelly was supposed to be provocative and fluttering her eyelashes. It was just so funny because we had thermal tops on and about seven hundred layers of clothes. I had opaque tights because they're supposed to make the skirt look shorter but instead of wearing one pair I had about four pairs on – it was so unflattering! When I watched it, my legs looked like a

Adele Silva (Kelly Windsor) recalls: 'When Kelly and Tom (Jeremy Turner-Welch) just got together, it was freezing cold in the stable and if you've noticed whenever *Emmerdale* does a sex scene, it always involves hay, one way or another!'

Kim's stable burns furiously in the aftermath of 1993's dramatic plane crash which boosted viewing figures and tested the skills of the special effects department

hippo!

'Even when Kelly and Tom first got together, it was freezing cold in the stable and if you've noticed whenever *Emmerdale* does a sex scene, it always involves hay, one way or another!' she laughs.

Alun Lewis who plays Kelly's dad Vic Windsor, wasn't laughing as he recalled how he too suffered the vagaries of the Yorkshire weather. 'My most memorable moment of filming was being up to the knees in a freezing mountain stream at Bolton Abbey – I was in a tor-

rential waterfall for three days, on and off, for about eight hours a day. I had a wet suit on but it was still cold. I was supposed to have caught my foot under a log under the water. I'll never forget that! It was in March, so you can imagine...'

His screen wife, Viv (Deena Payne) still remembers her first day on set. She had never met Alun Lewis in her life but his first words to her were 'Are you my wife?' 'Yes,' was her reply. 'Are you my husband?' Five minutes later they were being filmed walking through the village, having to act as though they'd been married for ten years.

Luckily, they hit it off together immediately.

Deena said of her screen family, 'We were a family straight away. We all got on really well – I think it was partly because we were the first new family they'd had on *Emmerdale* for four or five years so we were all in the same boat.'

Alun confesses he would normally have been quite nervous but didn't have time to think about it. 'The night before I'd been doing an episode of *Birds of a Feather* and it was such a rush having to get up to Yorkshire to film in the morning that nerves didn't come into it – I'd walked off one set and on to another!'

Paula Tilbrook, who plays busybody Betty Eagleton says she would never contemplate living in sin as Betty does with Seth. Nor could she see herself working in a wine bar. 'I've learned that I never want to work in a cafe – no way! Sometimes I'm in there on studio days almost half a day and I don't sit down any of the time. I know I don't want to be a waitress – it's too hard on the knees!'

Frank Tate and Viv Windsor battle with the flames in an effort to save the stables

Lisa (Jane Cox) gives Zak
(Steve Halliwell) a flash
of her garter following
their blessing in
September 1997

Probably the most dramatic event in the series' history came at the end of 1993 when a plane crashed, devastating much of the village and killing Mark Hughes, Elizabeth Felman, Archie Brooks and Leonard Kempinski.

'The air crash scene was absolutely freezing, bitterly cold and people were up to their waists in water,' remembers Keith Richardson. 'There was a lot of very difficult effects with the flames and I thought it all looked terrific. It cost us an arm and a leg! Not only did it boost viewing figures, it also boosted morale for the show. Often in a soap people get a bit despondent because they think theyíre treated as poor relations. But because we were investing so much time and money I think it gave the cast and the crew something to really get their teeth into.

'The whole episode took about three weeks from start to finish. It was the most memorable scene but it was a collage of memorable scenes – it wasn't just the crash. When Frank Tate discovered a baby in a tree, it was a very moving moment and when Jack Sugden found young Mark had been killed that was also moving.'

Despite the cast's recollections of being frozen to the bone on many occasions, only twice in 25 years has production stopped because of weather conditions. 'It can be freezing but we try to keep going in snow,' assures Keith. 'Snow did once grind us to a halt and we couldn't get the vehicles out. But if we can move things at all we keep going. Our schedule is such that we just don't have any built-in additional time.' From an original cast of only nine regular characters, there are now over thirty. The original line-up was Annie Sugden, Jack Sugden, Joe Sugden, Peggy Skilbeck, Matt Skilbeck, Sam Pearson, Henry Wilks, Marian Wilks and Amos Brierly.

Some people's faces have changed overnight when new actors have been chosen to play the same role - more than fifteen characters have been played by more than one actor/actress. Only the character of Jack Sugden has been there since the outset although he has been played by a different actor (Clive Hornby) since 1980.

Most recently, Sarah Sugden acquired a new persona when Alyson Spiro took over from Madeleine Howard in 1994. 'Sarah was missing from the show for six or seven episodes,' recalls Keith, 'and when she came back she looked substantially different but as long as you're up front about it, I think the viewers accept it.'

Alyson took to the part immediately but confesses there are few similarities between herself and her character, except for the fact that she has children of her own. 'I have three – Ella is

As Frank's solicitor (Alan Faulkner) begins the reading of the Will, Kim Tate (Claire King) is pretty confident of a beneficial outcome, but where would that leave Chris (Peter Amory) and Zoe (Leah Bracknell)?

six and Cara and Georgia are four but apart from that, we don't have much in common. I'm a Londoner and she was originally a Londoner but I don't think I could be a farmer's wife. Putting your hand up cows' bottoms is not for me!'

Stan Richards (Seth) who has been with the cast for nearly twenty years is the longest serving member. He gets through about 24 woolly hats in a year, most of which are given away to charity.

Richard Thorp, who plays landlord Alan Turner, remembers one of his funniest moments on set when he and Stan had a scene with Seth's dog...

'It was Stan's own dog. It wasn't used to being on set and it was terribly nervous and kept trying to run away. We wanted this dog sitting between us while we were talking so we attached it to the leg of my chair where the audience couldn't see the lead. At one stage I got carried away because I was ticking Seth off as usual, so I leaned across and lifted my bum from the chair. The dog chose that moment to bolt, and disappeared out of the door, taking the chair with it and I was left with nothing to sit on. We just cried with laughter...'

Since Alan took over The Woolpack in 1982, Richard is convinced that being a pub landlord in real life might be a bit too much like hard work!

'When we do a whole day's filming in The Woolpack from first thing in the morning until last thing at night, I suppose that must be a bit like a publican's day and by the end of it, I'm totally knackered!

'At least I know what I'm meant to be saying and what the customers are saying! I would imagine laughing at the same jokes for weeks on end must be a bit of a strain. All the landlords I've met because of the work I do are very likeable people. There's a sort of nice warmth about them. They're very street-wise and I like that. Yes, when I got the part of Alan Turner I felt it was my duty to research the Yorkshire pubs!'

The beginning of 1994 saw the rebuilding of Beckinsale in the wake of the air crash. Frank and Kim Tate remarried at the end of the year. Chris, Frank's son, was now in a wheelchair and his marriage to Kathy fell apart later in the year when she discovered he was having an affair with Rachel Hughes.

The same year saw the introduction of the Dingle family who now provide much of the light-hearted relief from the antics of scheming arch-bitch Kim Tate and the villagers' various affairs of the heart which always seem destined to end in tears. Ben and Butch were the first Dingles to grace our screens but it wasn't all comedy. Ben died during a row with Luke McAllister at a party and Luke was held responsible until it was subsequently discovered that Ben had a heart defect. The Dingles still blamed Luke however and were horrified when their sister Tina became involved with him – until she dumped him at the altar, announcing it had all been an act of revenge.

Since then, the Dingles have brought hilarity to the series as they lurch from one disastrous scam to another. Not surprisingly, most of the Dingles' wardrobe on set comes from car boot sales!

Biff Fowler, played by Stuart Wade, has seen very little comedy for his character – after a series of emotional upheavals, last year saw the death of his wife, Linda, played by Tonicha Jeronimo who is also his partner in real life.

Before Biff married Linda, Stuart remarked, 'I can only see the obvious likenesses between me and Biff – things like riding the bikes – and chasing the girls,' he joked. 'But I've got a theory that everybody in the cast has been picked because there's something there that's like their character.'

Filming normally takes place about six weeks ahead of transmission but deadlines can sometimes be even tighter when holidays come into the equation. It isn't unusual for the team to have three units working in different places on one day. However, production should become easier this year

with completion of the new purpose-built village on the outskirts of Leeds. 'We are currently creating an entire village in the grounds of Harewood estate,' explains Keith Richardson. 'Some sets will be there and some will be in the studio.'

The purpose-built set is the first of its kind in the UK with its own electricity supply and high tech security system. A hundred men will have worked six days a week for eighteen weeks to complete the project which covers 11 acres and incorporates half a mile of dry stone walling and 900 square miles of turf. A full time gardener is on hand to maintain the gardens which have been tailor made to suit each character. Special smoke machines have been installed to create a smoke effect from the chimneys and yoghurt placed on some roofs to encourage

lichen to grow and give the properties an old appearance. All along, the production team has worked in consultation with conservationists.

Emmerdale is the only soap with its own fan club, organising special weekends for members, as well as studio tours and dinners which are attended by as many of the artists as possible, giving the fans an opportunity to talk to the cast.

Of the future, Keith Richardson smiles, 'Obviously, we're looking forward to the next 25 years!'

For details of the Emmerdale Fan Club, write to:
The Emmerdale Club, PO BOX 33, St Albans, Herts AL4 0LF.
Members will receive regular newsletters packed with up to date
information about the programme and its stars.

Once used for industry, Yorkshire's waterways have enjoyed a major refurbishment in recent years and are now widely used for leisure pursuits and boat trips through *Emmerdale* country. For further information contact Bradford Waterways tel. 01274 611303
(LEEDS CITY COUNCIL)

2
THE DARLING BUDS
OF MAY

The larger-than-life Larkin family became the nation's darlings when they first romped through the Kent countryside and on to our screens in the summer of 1991.

For Pop, Ma and their brood of six children, life was 'Perfick... just perfick'. Set in the summer of 1958, the family never seemed to have a care in the world and the shine perpetually shone.

Says Richard Bates, executive producer, 'The series was based on the books by H.E. Bates who was my father. I had control of the rights to the books and it all started with a chance meeting with Vernon Lawrence who was head of entertainment at Yorkshire Television at the time. He was looking for a new project for David Jason following the success of *A Bit of a Do* and that's how Yorkshire became interested, although the series was actually set in Kent at the other end of the country.

'It was Vernon's enthusiasm for the book and working with David that made us realise we could put the two properties together so to speak and come up

The Larkin family – originally inspired by a man buying ice cream in a Kent village shop!

Location shot of farm and bungalow – the production crew had to make a few alterations with the addition of several items of junk which Pop Larkin eventually hoped to turn into a handsome profit

with a very successful series – although nobody at the time anticipated that it was going to be quite as successful as it was.'

When the first series went out in 1991, it created an extraordinary precedent by leaping straight to Number One in the ratings with its very first episode and staying there for the first series of six programmes – an achievement which was a first in the history of television. The programme consistently attracted viewing figures of between 17 and 18 million.

'That was an extraordinary response by the viewing public,' says Richard. 'It's very interesting that when we did research into the audience and responses we found that the demographic for *The Darling Buds* was actually a perfect match for the demographic of the country as a whole which explains why it did achieve nearly 18 million viewers. To get that top of the ratings figure you would have to appeal right across the entire spectrum.'

It was decided to adapt each book into two

one-hour episodes so that they could be screened as one-hour shows or turned into a two- hour TV movies to suit a longer slot in the schedule. Series One was later repeated as three two-hour films. In total, twenty one-hour pro-grammes were made, using four writers. Since the series finished, viewers have been able to watch repeats on ITV, Sky and UK Gold and an episode was screened after Princess Diana's funeral.

The inspiration for Pop Larkin came from a visit by H.E. Bates to a local Kent shop where he and his wife watched with astonishment as a man walked in and bought piles of ice cream with the biggest roll of bank notes they had ever seen. Back outside, he distributed the goodies to his huge family before they all drove off in a blue lorry. The author began to wonder about them on the way home – and the Larkins were born.

David Jason brought the character of Pop Larkin to flamboyant life as the entre-preneurial farmer-cum-junk-dealer with a heart of gold. One of the keys to the show's success was that it was great family entertainment. Said David at the time, of other

Pluckley Post Office
(JACK PLEASANT)

The Larkin family's happy lifestyle provided great family entertainment, the only whiff of scandal being the fact that Ma and Pa had never quite got around to marrying...

television shows, 'For my money there is too much sex and violence and not enough old-fashioned family entertainment. *The Darling Buds of May* seems to be the kind of television that is hardly seen any more.'

David also showed hidden talents in the role... When the script called for him to milk a cow for real, everybody thought a number of takes would be necessary before he got it right but he proved them all wrong and did it perfectly first time. It then came to light that he'd been taught to do it for a previous part.

The Darling Buds of May – a quote from a Shakespeare sonnet – was the title of the first book written by H.E. Bates, published in 1957. He then went on to write four sequels which have never been out of print. 'They've become in their own way a sort of classic,' says Richard.

'My father would work in the garden for nine months, and during that time he would be writing a novel in his head.

'He once told me that by the time he came to sit down and write the book, he knew every word of it in his mind. But the sheer mental concentration in getting it down on paper was like giving birth to a baby. I once went into his study when he was working. He was writing, but the paper was blank because his pen had run out and he hadn't noticed.'

The village which YTV finally chose for the location was the Kent village of Pluckley. Says Richard, 'It happens to be the very next village to where my parents lived and where I was born so that's exactly the area my father was writing about. Then it was a question of visiting a lot of farms in the area to find something which we felt was suitable and an owner who was willing to be invaded for the next three years.'

Pluckley also has another claim to fame – it is said to be Britain's most haunted village but the only spirits seen by the cast were likely to have been those served behind the bar at the village

Mariette and Charley in the strawberry field – the setting for one of Mariette's most memorable scenes when she had to fight off a rival for Charley's affections

Mariette, Charley and 'Baby John' who was played by Daisy May Bates, the real life granddaughter of H. E. Bates

Filming on location

local, The Black Horse, which appeared on our screens as The Hare and Hounds.

'For the farm, it was a question of whittling down a list of possible properties and we lighted upon Home Farm as being the appropriate one. We didn't make any alterations but we brought in quite a bit of rubbish! Pop Larkin's yard is full of scrap metal and old agricultural bits and pieces which one day he's convinced he'll sell and make a profit on. So we brought in a few bits and pieces but we didn't attempt to make any major changes.'

The weather always appeared to be glorious in the series. Richard recalls, 'Remarkably, the first year of filming was 1990 and it was not a very good summer. I was working in my office only forty miles from where they were filming. On many occasions I thought they'll have stopped filming as it's a dull day or it's raining – then I would phone the set at the end of the day to see how they were getting on and they had had perfect sunshine. If you look at the first series it's extraordinary that although it wasn't a very good summer elsewhere they were blessed

(Right)
Darling Buds of May
country – a tranquil
scene at Pluckley
(JACK PLEASANT)

(Below)
Wherever the Larkins
gathered, food – in plen-
tiful supply – was never
far away

by endless sunshine. Someone was looking down on them.'

When part of the series was filmed in
Brittany, tour operators found themselves inundated with requests for
brochures for tourists hoping to emulate
the Larkin lifestyle.

Although the Larkins needed a holiday, Pop isn't at all sure about setting
foot on foreign soil and eating all that
foreign food. But Charley speaks French
and remembers idyllic sunny pre-war
holidays at the Hotel Beau Rivage in
Brittany. The family pile into Pa's pride
and joy – his immaculate yellow vintage
Rolls Royce – and arrive in France only
to find that Charley's remembered idyll
doesn't quite come up to scratch. The
hotel is shabby, the weather wild and
the food and drink are far from meeting
Pa's standards. And the hotel manage-
ment are disapproving of having an
unmarried couple – Ma and Pa – sharing
a room.

During filming, the cast even man-
aged to fall foul of some of the real

locals. Philip Franks (Charley) was playing a drunk scene on a little French country railway station, with the camera out of sight, when a cafe owner suddenly appeared at an upstairs window shouting that she wasn't going to have any drunks in her house! She rushed downstairs and locked all the doors before anyone could explain to her what was happening.

The hapless Charley was often the victim of Larkin excesses and once woke up at Home Farm feeling very much the worse for wear. Pop insisted that he down a 'Larkins' Special' – complete with raw egg – as a hangover cure. 'It

really was revolting,' recalls Philip, 'and I had to drink it down in one go. Talk about suffering for the sake of art. It was disgusting.'

Catherine Zeta Jones, the Welsh beauty who played Mariette, is named after a Greek battleship! She takes the name 'Zeta' from her grandmother, whose father named his daughter after the battleship he served on – *The Zeta*.

Catherine had to film some of the series with a broken arm. During one of the gymkhana scenes her horse bolted and though experienced rider Catherine clung on for dear life, she finally fell, knocking herself unconscious and cracking

Filming always seemed to be blessed by endless summer sunshine – Pop entertains Victoria (Stephanie Ralph) and Oscar (Ross Marriot)

The adult Larkins

a bone in her arm.

Millions of viewers were moved to tears when Mariette finally married Cedric, the mild-mannered tax inspector nicknamed Charley by the Larkin family. 'Nothing but the best for the most beautiful girl in Kent,' insisted Pop, 'Mariette is going to look like a queen.' It was set to be the wedding of the year and the day was going to be 'perfick'.

The little church at Pluckley was packed out for the fictitious marriage and one of the wedding 'guests' was Mrs Madge Bates, widow of the author.

Another member of the Bates family also appeared in the series. Daisy May Bates, baby granddaughter of H.E. Bates, made her acting debut – as a boy – when Mariette and Charley had their first baby, John Blenheim.

One of Catherine's most memorable scenes was when she had to fight off a rival for the affections of Charley when they were first courting. The rough and tumble in the strawberry field was pretty realistic, leaving Catherine with squashed strawberries in her hair, in her ears and even up her nose! She says, 'I've always been cast as a bit of a goody-goody and having a fight like that was something I've always wanted to do.'

For Richard Bates, one of his favourite moments in the book was of Ma and Pa sharing a bath together. 'That was a wonderful moment on television,' he remembers, 'it was a very funny scene.'

Pam Ferris was a big star in every sense of the word and willingly agreed to pile on two stone to play the happy-go-lucky roly-poly Ma Larkin – but she still needed extra padding to reach the required ample measurements – a 50 inch bust and 50 inch hips!

But she had certain reservations about that bath scene – until David Jason put her at ease by waddling on to the set resplendent in face-mask, snorkel and a huge pair of flippers, shouting, 'I'm ready for the bath scene – are you ready, Pam?'

Playing Ma Larkin was a role Pam enjoyed – immensely! 'She was a joy to play because she's such a wonderful woman, so full of love, happiness and

A glimpse of the Kent countryside – the Larkins' rural idyll
(JACK PLEASANT)

The Larkin brood – the
'perfick' family

humour.'

Pam and Ma Larkin also share a common interest – cooking. Pam laughs, 'I certainly knew what I was doing in the kitchen scenes but I never thought that being able to truss a chicken correctly would one day come in handy in my acting career.'

The food wasn't always palatable. A vegetarian, Pam had to forgo her principles and eat meat – lots of it – for the sake of authenticity and there is one scene she'll never forget... 'Once we had to do a scene where David and I were munching chocolate and pickled onions in bed. Then, another day, we re-shot the scene with kippers. I never want to see another kipper in my life!'

Perhaps the biggest compliment to Pam came from the author's widow who visited the set as filming was in progress. Mrs Bates' face lit up as she saw Pam and she cried, 'That's it! That IS Ma Larkin!'

Says Richard: 'It was part of my role to see that we didn't deviate from the books too much but the books lent themselves – they're very visual and the characters are very clearly defined and it wasn't difficult to adapt them. Then when we had finished adapting the five books I went on to devise some original stories with our writers so that we could extend the series for further episodes.'

When it came to food and drink, the Larkins lived like kings. Richard laughs, 'I think Pam Ferris made the most of the opportunities! Our location caterers were given the responsibility of providing the food for the set – cooking two or three geese for lunch and I'm sure it all got eaten up by the end of the day. The cast and crew had a very good time...'

So why did the series finish when everybody appeared to be enjoying themselves and it was still one of the most popular series on our screens?

Says Richard, 'The difficulty was that we started out with one well known television star and very good actors and actresses and by the time we had finished the first series we had four television stars who were nationally known figures and in the end we couldn't hold the cast together. They understandably wanted to go off and do their own thing. We'd done twenty hours which we thought was pretty good and I don't think we shall be bringing them back together again. But that's the reality of life...'

The North Yorks Moors
has its own starring role
in *Heartbeat*. At a pre-
view of the series, the
audience said they were
disappointed the pro-
gramme hadn't shown
more countryside, so that
was quickly rectified.
(SCARBOROUGH BOROUGH
COUNCIL)

3
HEARTBEAT

Heartbeat arose from a series of books written under the pen-name of Nicholas Rhea, about a young village constable in the Yorkshire Dales. The author, Peter Walker, had retired from the police force as an inspector in charge of public relations and decided to concentrate on his writing.

Keith Richardson, Controller of Drama at YTTV says, 'At the time we (Yorkshire Television) were looking for something new and we'd had these book options for quite a long time. In order to make the programme acceptable up and down the country, we thought it would be good to explore the attitudes of locals to somebody coming from the south, which is a departure from the books. We did use the books as a basis but we mucked them about a bit.'

The team began to look for the right actor for the role of Nick Rowan. They wanted a recognised name and Nick Berry had already proved his popularity in *Eastenders*.

'From the moment I met Nick Berry I knew he was the one,' recalls Keith.

In order to create some real drama it was felt

Nick Berry had already proved his popularity in *Eastenders* before landing the part of PC Nick Rowan

The North York Moors and the coastline were deliberately chosen, rather than the Dales because of the contrasting scenery. Whitby could be 'Strensford', the fictional seaside town in the series.
(SCARBOROUGH BOROUGH COUNCIL)

that the country bobby needed a spirited partner. Rowan's wife in the original books was a traditional housewife, looking after her husband and children but as doctors tend to work alongside police and vice versa it was decided that giving him a doctor as a wife would be a good device for storytelling. It also spawned the title. '*Heartbeat* was originally called *Country Constable*,' remembers Keith, 'which sounded

like a series about art.'

Niamh Cusack was cast to play Nick's wife, Kate. 'They were good together from the start. They looked right as a couple and there was a spark between them. Once we had got those two the rest just carried on.'

A small test audience who had been treated to an advance preview said they were a bit disappointed that the programme hadn't shown

more countryside so the emphasis
was changed to include more of
the spectacular views on location.

Undoubtedly, the countryside
has played a huge part in the success of the series. When searching
for a location for Aidensfield,
Goathland and the North
Yorkshire Moors were quite deliberately chosen, rather than the
Dales because it was somewhere
which had rarely been featured on
television before.

'You get an interesting contrast
there – the purple heather and
there's green and soft landscape as
well. The wind comes off the
North Sea there and it can be very
cold.'

The unpredictable weather pre-
sents the usual problems for the
film crew. 'We don't really mind if
weather is one thing or the other
– if it's dull, that's fine, if it's
sunny, that's fine but if you get
ten minutes of one and half an
hour of the other, that's hopeless!
Where we are, the weather
alters very quickly so we spend
a lot of time waiting for it to
change.'

The pub scenes were originally
filmed in a hotel in Goathland.
'We used to use the real interior
of the pub but eventually we were
there too long and we interfered
with the chap's business too much
so it was recreated as a set.
Likewise, Nick's house. We start-

Schoolteacher Jo Weston
(Juliette Gruber) who
became Nick's second
wife after first wife, Kate,
died of leukaemia

Egton Moor – the cast of *Heartbeat* all say how much they enjoy being on location in such a beautiful part of the country (SCARBOROUGH BOROUGH COUNCIL)

ed with a real house and ended up recreating it in the studio. We did the same with the police station.'

When the programme was first broadcast on Friday, 10th April, 1992, initial audience responses were terrific. The series then moved to Sundays after the first series. Recent viewing figures revealed that more people watch *Heartbeat* then an average heart beats in six months! The highest figures achieved were 18.7 million, knocking *Coronation Street* off the Number One spot.

Set in the Sixties, the combination of gentle nostalgia and strong storylines make compulsive viewing. As Nick Berry said, '*Heartbeat* is all about 'the good old days' – which probably never existed, but it's nice to think they did.' Nevertheless, viewers who are tired of the

crime-hit rat race of the Nineties are happy to turn to the programme for some light-hearted escapism.

'People keep asking me what I think is the reason for the programme's success,' says Keith Richardson. 'I think it's a whole lot of things. Nick was a huge part of it but there's an ensemble of players there. I don't think it's changed much except we've made sure where previously it was all Nick and his wife, it's now more the whole set of characters. We've tried to write to ensure everybody gets a decent whack in each episode.

'You've got Greengrass – and the other guys in the police station are great value. It has created a franchise which is *Heartbeat* Country

(Left)
Kazia Pelka (District nurse Maggie Bolton)

(Below)
Goathland Station – visitors to the area should take the opportunity to enjoy a trip on the North Yorkshire Moors Railway, catching the train at Pickering or Grosmont near Whitby for the 18 mile journey through *Heartbeat* country (SCARBOROUGH BOROUGH COUNCIL)

(Right)
Greengrass (Bill
Maynard) is at home
down on the farm

(Below)
Claude lands himself in
another scrape

and I think the music plays a huge part. It's a format which has been copied by a number of programmes since but not so successfully.'

There wasn't a dry eye in the house when Nick's wife Kate died of leukaemia, leaving Nick to bring up baby Katie alone. But with the help of Auntie Eileen (Anne Stallybrass) he began to take part in village life again. Nobody was more delighted than Auntie Eileen when Nick found new romance with schoolteacher Jo Weston, played by Juliette Gruber.

Said Anne at the time, 'Eileen's very keen on this new relationship. There was somebody in the last series that she wasn't keen on at all but when she meets Jo, she senses straight away that this might be the right one. I think she's intuitive in that way.'

Auntie Eileen, of course, turned out to be right. Nick and Jo eventually married, but only after a few ups and downs in their relationship. Juliette said of working with Nick, 'Because I do most of my scenes with him, it could have been a nightmare, (if they hadn't got on well) 'but he's just lovely and so easy to work with.'

Nick, reputedly Britain's highest paid actor, said last year, 'The crew are as much a part of the success of the show as everybody else and everything else. They've been here since the start and they're here first and last every day and we just turn up and do the good bits. We socialise all the time together. We have this football team, girls excluded at the moment – a few honorary girlies but it's mostly the lads. The joy of this job is being here and being with this crew. They've been wonderful to us.'

He added, 'Life at the police station seems to reflect life as it was and still is in certain rural stations. The crime wave in Aidensfield is worse

The spectacular glacial gorge of Newtondale in the heart of *Heartbeat* country
(SCARBOROUGH BOROUGH COUNCIL)

Flo (Patricia Hayes) in
'Expectations', an
episode from Series Five

than New York now.'

Nick's dour-faced police sergeant, Oscar Blaketon – now the village postmaster – was always ready to present the young constable with new challenges. Derek Fowlds has a more cheerful disposition than his character and for five years was better known as 'Mr Derek' in a double act with Basil Brush! 'If we want to be recognised we go out with Nick because they mob him. When Jo arrived we were all extremely

attracted to her immediately – especially Ventress and Bellamy. I thought Blaketon stood a chance but obviously he's slightly over the hill.'

Mark Jordon who plays Bellamy chips in : 'I think Bellamy's a bit jealous as well because Jo's quite a stunner and I think he would have liked to have found her first... I'm not too sure if Bellamy's ever going to get a girl. He seems to be the most disastrous relationship-maker in the world. Secretly, I think he'll always have a bit of a passion for Gina (landlady of The Aidensfield Arms) but I don't think she's interested because she knows him too well – and she knows he's a plonker.'

On being part of the cast, he says, 'It's the luckiest job I've ever done. Everybody's so sweet – apart from me, obviously. Everyone will tell you I'm the boil on everybody's backside but there's got to be one, hasn't there? There's lots of bonding – beer and bonding – it's perfect for me, that!'

Ventress is the other member of the local police force. William Simons says of his character Ventress, 'He doesn't really like spending too long in the police station but I think he prefers that to spending too long at home!'

One of the longest running problems for the team has been trying to keep the old Francis Barnett motorcycle going which tends to pour blue smoke from its exhaust.

Nick smiles. 'I never fell off the bike but it's so slow I'm sure I wouldn't have hurt myself anyway. I was once overtaken by some sheep, so it's not the fastest of bikes but I loved it just the same.'

Nick is reputed to have cried real tears as he left Aidensfield for good. As PC Nick Rowan sets off for Canada to join the Mounties, Claude Greengrass, the village rogue, has the last word, 'Try not to fall off your horse!'

Bill Maynard, who plays Claude Greengrass, sums up another reason why the show is such a winner. 'You can gauge it by the guest artists who come. Every one of them says they've never known such a wonderful atmosphere.'

Bill is recognised everywhere he goes but takes it all in his stride. 'I've worked for many many years to make my face instantly recognisable, and I don't see why, having done that, I should try and hide myself.'

Bill's constant companion on set is Alfred, Claude's dog. 'As far as Alfred is concerned, of course, he's not only his best friend, he's a son.'

Nick and Jo before they leave Aidensfield for pastures new

(Right)
North Yorkshire`Moors
Railway
(SCARBOROUGH BOROUGH
COUNCIL)

(Below)
Blaketon and Auntie
Eileen come to grips with
the finer points of golf

Alfred isn't his real name – he's like all other
members of equity! If I call him Alfred he does-
n't come so I call him son a lot so he doesn't
get too confused about his different names. He
is the most wonderful dog I think I have ever
met.'

Nobody quite knows, least of all Bill, exactly
what Greengrass's next scam is going to be but
he says with a twinkle in his eye, 'You never
know, one of these days, Claude might have a
shave, put a clean shirt on and take Maggie out
for a meal – who knows what might develop. I
mean, anything could happen...'

District nurse Maggie Bolton, played by
Kazia Pelka was pleased when Nick and Jo got
together. 'Jo confides in Maggie about the relationship and I think my character sees it as a
good thing for Nick.

Nurse Maggie and Bellamy cope with another drama in Aidensfield

'I don't think Maggie ever harboured any secret thoughts towards Nick, other than as a good friend, and because she was so close to Kate – and Nick – they became closer because they both shared the experience of Kate dying.

'Also, for the sake of Katie she thinks Jo's influence is a good one. And of course, Maggie's got Greengrass!'

She laughs as she remembers one occasion when she was recognised. 'I was in the supermarket, looking rather smart actually. A woman said, "It is her, look I told you it was. She's not as pretty in real life, is she?" The other one said, "No, she's not as tall either..."'

After the first series, most of the storylines

Mike Bradley, played by Jason Durr, is already a popular addition to the series. Will he take over as top *Heartbeat* heart-throb?

from the Constable books had been used and so it was up to the scriptwriters to devise new material. As time went on, the stories gradually became less 'cosy' and harder-hitting than Peter Walker's original books.

The biggest stunt was a train crash in the snow in an episode called *Riders of the Storm*. The actual crash was shown and then scenes of the carriage turned on its side and the aftermath.

As well as stunts, special effects are often required. Says Keith Richardson, 'We're usually asked to do a Christmas episode in July or August and obviously Christmas should have snow so we find ourselves artificially creating snow and laying it all over the place – so that's always fun.

'I think one of the best episodes was one we did about foot and mouth disease. It was called *Bitter Harvest*. It was something people had forgotten about which used to be the scourge of the countryside. It shocked some people who

didn't realise it was as difficult as it was. I think the playing of it and the fact that we used the soundtrack *Knights in White Satin* made it very, very moving as the farmer watched all his cattle being slaughtered.'

PC Mike Bradley, played by Sharpe actor Jason Durr has already joined the force at Ashfordly police station but PC Mike Bradley is a very different character from Nick.

'I think the changes will work quite nicely,' says Keith Richardson. 'When Niamh left we wondered whether the public would take to the show without her but it created an opportunity to investigate how a young man copes with looking after a child on his own so it opened up the storytelling. The same may happen with Nick going. We can tell different stories yet still with the same community feel.

'Because Mike Bradley's not a married man and doesn't have a child the show will be different… maybe more sexy?'

46

View east from Plockton,
West Highlands,
Scotland
(GRAHAM JENNINGS)

4
HAMISH MACBETH

O ff -beat bobby Hamish Macbeth is responsible for keeping law and order in the tiny village of Lochdhu where major crime isn't too much of a problem but bending the law is a way of life.

However excellent his policing skills, which rarely follow conventional procedures, Hamish has only one great ambition – to avoid promotion at all costs. That would mean leaving his home in Lochdubh and his faithful canine companion, Wee Jock. Besides, Hamish is a great believer in 'live and let live'.

But with his nearest superior officers based over a hundred miles away, Hamish is pretty safe to carry on with his unconventional lifestyle and unorthodox methods of solving crime.

'He sees himself as the sheriff of a one-horse town,' explains Robert Carlyle, who plays Hamish. 'To him, Lochdubh is the

Hamish Macbeth (Robert Carlyle) has his own unique style of keeping law and order

Hamish with Laurie Ventry who plays the Reverend Snow

Wild West and he has his own way of dealing with crimes and misdemeanors. I like Hamish,' he adds, 'because he isn't afraid to show his gentler side and he has no ambition whatsoever.

'He's a maverick, a law unto himself, and I think people find that attractive. He's a figure of authority but in Lochdubh his authority is maintained by who he is, not what he is. He's not a squeaky-clean policeman – that's the attraction. He's scabby, he's dry and he follows his instincts. That's the man – and that's the

character the audience responded to.'

Wherever Hamish goes, Wee Jock is never far behind and he has been known to jealously guard Hamish's bed whenever an attractive woman is in town.

In the first series, Wee Jock was played by Zippy, a West Highland terrier from Dumfries. It was Zippy's first television series and producer Deirdre Kerr praises his acting talents: 'He had to prick up his ears, look lively, follow Hamish devotedly, act jealous, growl menacingly and

The promontory where
the police station was
located
(GRAHAM JENNINGS)

Lachie Junior (Stuart
Davids) and Lachie (Billy
Riddoch)

bark on command. Once he understood his motivation, Zippy was a one-take performer.'

Zippy was trained for the series by David Stewart of Creature Features, suppliers of animals to the film industry. 'Westies are quite excitable and aren't that easy to train,' says Dave and explains that he was looking for one which would not only respond to commands but which had bags of personality. A sure-fire way of grabbing Zippy's attention was to produce his favourite squeaky toy.

'When Zippy heard it, he went berserk,'

remembers Dave. 'On the first day of filming, Zippy was ready for his big scene in Hamish's land-rover. His coat was all white and fluffy and clean. I squeaked the toy to get his attention and he jumped straight out of the window and landed, face down, in a muddy puddle.'

Sadly, in the first series, Wee Jock met a grisly fate at the hands of a hit-and-run driver and Hamish was inconsolable until he was presented with a new puppy to care for – Wee Jock Two, played by Fraoch (Gaelic for Heather).

'Frew' was discovered by Dave Stewart in Fort William after first being spotted by

Hollywood actress Jessica Lange who fell for the little dog while filming *Rob Roy*. Although Fraoch was a newcomer to television, he immediately took to his acting role and the attendant public adulation with great enthusiasm. So much so, that Dave had to make sure he conserved the pup's energies for filming.

In the third series, some of the scenes demanded the skills of a specifically trained film dog so while Fraoch was working on the less demanding scenes, Dexter from London was

Hamish was confronted by a choice between the love of two women – Alex (Valerie Gogan) and Isobel (Shirley Henderson) until a tragic twist of fate dictated the outcome

Rory (Brian Pettipher), Isobel (Shirley Henderson), Lachlan (Billy Riddoch), Hamish (Robert Carlyle) and Doc Brown (Duncan Duff)

being trained by Gill Raddings who also trains Wellard in *Eastenders*, Timmy in *The Famous Five* and has worked on *101 Dalmatians*.

Whereas Hamish returned to his Highland roots because he was disillusioned with city life, Robert is very much a city dweller, born and bred in Glasgow, and he approached the prospect of the first three month shoot in such a remote location with some trepidation. 'I can't deny I missed city life,' he admits, 'but living in

a village with a population of only two hundred was quite an eye-opener. People have time for one another and I realised that community spirit is what gets them through the long dark winter.'

Inspired by the books of MC Beaton and adapted by scriptwriter Danny Boyle, the greatest appeal of the series was probably its black humour and strong characterisation. As Robert himself pointed out, there are a number of characters sufficiently fascinating in their own right to justify the focus of a whole episode which meant he didn't feel he was a one-man show.

The close-knit community of Lochdubh features a colourful crowd of inhabitants including TV John (Ralph Riach), so called because he owned the very first TV in Lochdubh. Hamish's friend and right-hand man, he is endowed with the gift of second sight; father and son ne'er-do-wells Lachlan (Billy Riddoch) local crofter, handyman and would-be entrepeneur and Lachie Junior (Stuart Davids) who is in charge of the local funeral parlour; Doctor Dougal Brown (Duncan Duff) Hamish's friend and confidant, with whom he often shares a drink and a smoke at the end of the day; the proprietor of the local store, Rory Campbell (Brian Pettifer) who lives alone above his shop, complete with silk sheets and a Jacuzzi and who is conducting a not-so-secret affair with Esme (Ann Lacey) the statuesque and voluptuous widow who teaches at the local school. Then there's Barney and Agnes Meldrum (Stuart McGugan and Barbara Rafferty) landlord and lady of The Lochdubh Hotel, local watering hole and the hub of village life.

Very different form the run-of-the-mill television police drama, neither was *Hamish Macbeth* an excuse to set a twee series in a picturesque setting.

The first series attracted 10 million viewers and when it went on air in March 1995, Robert was in Bristol filming the BBC drama *Go Now*.

He admits to being taken aback by the immediate success of *Hamish Macbeth*.

'I was stunned by the reaction of the public in Bristol,' he remembers. 'Although I knew that we were getting ten million viewers, you don't really understand what that means. The instant recognition of me in the street after just two episodes told me that people all over the country were watching.

'It was a big surprise. You just never know what an audience is going to like. I always had great confidence in the series – I wouldn't have taken the job if I hadn't believed in it. But I had absolutely no idea it was going to take off the way it did.'

However, not all viewers were enthralled. Real police officers were upset that the public would see the pot-smoking, laid back Hamish as an accurate portrayal of a real Highland police-men, Northern Constabulary even issuing a statement to the effect that the programme was light entertainment and should be regarded as such. The Scottish parody – stereotypes such as shortbread-tin tartan in the opening credits, the West Highland terrier, the Highland cattle – might be taken at face value by some viewers who didn't quite get the joke, but then, that was their problem. And in any case, the cliché of the Highland cattle was perfectly genuine. A herd does have right of way through the village, often causing a halt in filming.

The location for Lochdubh was not chosen lightly. 'We looked at practically every village on the west coast of Scotland,' recalls Deirdre Kerr. 'We had very particular requirements and Plockton fitted the bill perfectly. It's extraordinarily beautiful, it's not on a main road and it has the same kind of tight-knit community as Lochdubh.'

In fact, the programme makers covered twelve hundred miles of coastline before coming across Plockton and deciding immediately that it had all the right ingredients – perfect scenery, enough accommodation for up to ninety cast and technicians, a village shop, village hall, sailing club and plenty of volunteers as extras.

The village lies in a sheltered inlet just across the sea from Skye. It enjoys spectacular views across Loch Carron and the surrounding area of Wester Ross and because its climate is influenced by the Gulf Stream, incongruous palm trees fringe the harbour. Life there proceeds at a very unhurried pace, far from the intrusion of mobile phones which won't work in the area and without even a through road.

In the real life 'Lochdubh' the locals were made well aware that a certain amount of that peace and tranquility would be shattered by the invasion of a film crew and subsequent sightseers but they were also astute enough to realise that the attendant publicity would be good for business and gave the programme makers the go ahead.

Five miles' drive from Glasgow where most of the cast and crew had their homes, two hours from the nearest airport and shopping centre at Inverness and without the usual pre-requisites such as walkie-talkies and mobile phones which are usually needed to meet filming deadlines, the crew quickly realised that there was no alternative but to adjust to the local pace of life. Filming was often delayed by the procession of cattle along the high street and although there was very little traffic, large film trucks and buses had their work cut out negotiating roads which were better suited to sheep.

Certain changes had to be made to transform Plockton into Lochdubh. Hamish Macbeth's home-cum-police-station is a holiday home owned by a doctor from Glasgow. When a London family turned up for a pre-booked week's holiday, they were a bit taken aback to find their holiday cottage adorned with a blue lamp and bars at the window and a police cell where there should have been a bedroom but were perfectly happy to spend their week behind bars.

Plockton's newsagent, Edmund McKenzie, found his premises converted into Lochdubh general store and accommodatingly agreed to move his shop into the sailing club next door for each three months in which filming took place. So convincing was the Lochdubh store that one lady visitor asked the crew for clothes pegs.

The store lies on the corner where Wee Jock was killed by the getaway car and Edmund and Irene MacKenzie are often asked to point out the exact spot. Business is brisk selling souvenirs for tourists who want to take home a memento of the programme.

Hamish's watering hole, The Stag Bar in The Lochdubh Hotel is not within the 'hotel' we see on screen. The outside of the 'hotel' is a private house and the real Stag Bar is a few miles further along the road in the public bar of The Balmacara Hotel where the bar has been renamed The Stag Bar after the fictional pub. Confused? Perhaps you need a drink...

Plockton is very proud of its association with the famous series and the inhabitants agree that a little disruption is a small price to pay. Besides, they were compensated for their cooperation and the production even made a contribution to the village hall restoration project. 'The village hall is heavily featured in our series,' Deirdre points out, 'so it's nice to think that it will benefit directly from our presence. We used it to film a traditional ceilidh which most of the village took part in and was also the scene of

Rory (Brian Pettipher),
local shopkeeper

rehearsals for Lochdubh's own version of *West Side Story*.'

Plockton had attracted film crews before but when the *Hamish Macbeth* team returned to Plockton in the summer of 1995, they found themselves in the middle of the tourist boom generated by the first series. Even Heather, one of the Highland cows, had found some unwarranted attention from tourists a bit much to take. When her owners, Dolan and Anne MacKenzie discovered some tourists sitting their child on her back, they decided enough was enough and dispatched her to quieter pastures on the Isle of Skye.

Swelling the numbers in the village from two hundred local residents was an influx of tourists from as far afield as Australia, anxious to see the famous landmarks on Hamish's beat. In July and August, Plockton also hosts the annual sailing regatta so by the time the seventy cast and crew arrived, the village was bursting at the seams for three months – and the two local pubs found their number of regulars substantially increased. At The Creag-Nan-Darach Hotel, instead of business trailing off towards the end of the summer season, trade had doubled.

Loch Carron, Wester Ross
(HUGH WEBSTER, SCOTTISH HIGHLAND PHOTO LIBRARY)

The location crew made their HQ at Duncraig Castle which overlooks the bay.

'We became part of the community,' says Deirdre. 'We had to understand and respect village life in the same way that Hamish Macbeth does. After all, the village could do without us but we couldn't do without the village.'

Children from the community were auditioned as extras and a number of locals roped in to act as runners, assistants and drivers. Local B&B establishments did a roaring trade and the pub extended its mealtimes to fit in with the film schedule.

Robert often found himself being mistaken for a real policeman. 'I was regularly asked for directions to the nearest camp site,' he laughs, 'and several times people asked me whether the filming was a headache for the police. I usually just smiled and said it's no bother.'

The distinctions between reality and fiction often became blurred to the extent that local children had to be reminded to call him Bobby rather than Hamish.

In 1996 when the first two series were shown in Australia, a Wee Jock Appreciation Society was formed, a *Hamish Macbeth* page was set up on the Internet for fans and debates were held on national TV and radio as to whether the series should have subtitles. At the time, Robert said it was likely that the mail waiting for him on the Internet would remain unread. 'I don't know anything about the Internet,' he confessed.

One of the real debates amongst fans was whether Hamish would choose long-time love Isobel, played by Shirley Henderson or Alex, the snooty blonde bombshell, played by Valerie Grogan. In an unexpected twist to the plot, Alex was tragically killed in a car crash. Even the cast didn't know what the outcome was going to be and Deirdre Kerr's children were offered bribes at school to reveal the outcome but it was kept a closely guarded secret.

A far cry from his tough roles in the past in *Cracker*, the BBC drama *Go Now*, the lover of a gay priest in *Priest*, the psychotic Begbie in *Trainspotting* and his brilliant comedy role in *The Full Monty*, Robert enjoyed playing the gentle, contented character of Hamish but says it was a conscious decision to quit while they were ahead.

'We'd all basically decided before we even started that three series would be enough," says Robert. "That's not to say that I won't miss Hamish. He's been a smashing character to play.'

'I loved my time in Plockton,' he adds. 'There's a real community spirit you rarely find in the city. After four months, I didn't want to leave.'

Can we expect a return to our screens of *Hamish Macbeth* sometime in the future, perhaps even for a one-off special? More than 10 million fans would certainly like to think so...

5
BALLYKISSANGEL

The tale of an English catholic priest working in a tiny Irish parish might not seem to be the stuff of high viewing figures but after only three episodes, *Ballykissangel* became a hit series, attracting 15 million viewers.

When Father Peter Clifford arrives in the small Irish village of Ballykissangel, he finds himself the object of intense curiosity by the local inhabitants who are surprised to find themselves with a young, English curate.

Peter finds himself quickly absorbed into the community's lifestyle and does his best to cope with the villagers' long-established ways despite having to face a certain amount of opposition along the way.

'One thing this country needs is priests from England,' is the sarcastic observation of Assumpta Fitzgerald, the attractive yet stubborn landlady of the local pub.

Peter is played by Stephen Tompkinson whose previous roles included Damien Day in *Drop the Dead Donkey*.

'Father Clifford is a great character although he couldn't be more different from Damien if he tried,' observes Stephen. 'Peter Clifford is a young priest who spent three years in an inner-city parish in Manchester before being transferred to the village of Ballykissangel. He's a very determined young man, with tremendously strong faith. He doesn't have much truck with the old, traditional style of doing things, so consequently has a few run-ins with the old parish priest, Father MacAnally.'

Niall Toibin says of his character, 'Father MacAnally's probably a bit old-fashioned, even by the standards of older priests nowadays. He's even got a rooted objection to cremation, for instance.

'He's a bit of a schemer; he's as much of a politician as any of the elected ones. His interests would sometimes coincide with Quigley's (Brian Quigley, the village's sharp-operating local businessman), but he's devious and can be very clever in the way that he can be either for

Assumpta Fitzgerald
(Dervla Kirwan),
Ballykissangel landlady,
outside Fitzgerald's the
family pub she has
looked after since the
death of her mother

Avoca Handweavers, (established in 1723) Ireland's oldest mill, Avoca village, Co. Wicklow
(GEORGE HORNER)

or against Quigley, depending on his own objectives and what he sees as the Church's interests. I suppose what's most important is that he'd always be in favour of not rocking the boat. He's usually quite sardonic and can be very sarcastic.'

Stephen adds, 'Father Mac is jerking his chain in one direction and Peter's determined to go another way. He's a lot more lenient than some of the more traditional priests, as you discover through the story.'

It is his lenient tendencies which tend to pro-voke the more conservative members of his congregation, such as the village shopkeeper and self-appointed moral guardian, Kathleen Coner.

Stephen feels that the villagers' initial reticence is 'not so much because he's an Englishman but much more that he's been brought up in the city. This is a country environment, with everything that involves. Very often things are not what they seem on the surface.'

Peter also finds himself at loggerheads with Brian Quigley played by Irish actor Tony Doyle. Tony felt that the timing of the series was right for a light-hearted drama. 'There's been so much bad news over the last 25 years, but the outlook does seem to be brighter these days, and I'm very pleased that we're now getting different kinds of stories, like *Ballykissangel*. It's a lot of fun and I think we've avoided anything too excessively broad.'

The writing is warm and witty but subtle at the same time. Niall points out, 'This is a comedy only in so far as the comedy arises out of the characters, and the characters are so well drawn that the situations that develop may be comic.

Kieran Prendiville's scripts are superb and very, very real. Funny, but in a totally unforced way.'

Like any small Irish village, 'Ballykay' as the natives call it has more than its fair share of characters, gossip and intrigue. Locals are inclined to lay bets on the outcome of any situation as the hapless Peter discovers when he faces his driving test.

As the series develops, Father Peter becomes more and more of an accepted fixture in village life and his alliance with Assumpta and the prospect of forbidden love has kept viewers

Main street in Avoca
(GEORGE HORNER)

Soibhan (Deidre Donnelly), Eamonn (Birdy Sweeney) and Brendan (Gary Whelan)

guessing.

'He's quite a good match for Assumpta, who's equally determined, so they get along well, even though originally she didn't like men, priests or the English! Between him and Assumpta they solve various problems that happen to the villagers. They get on together, but itíll never be a question of "will they, won't they?"'

Dervla was easily persuaded to return to her native Ireland for the role of Assumpta. Brought up in a convent school just outside Dublin, she spent the first eighteen years of her life in Ireland.

Having recently been on our screens as Cockney landlady Phoebe in the hit series *Goodnight Sweetheart*, she says, 'It was great to be back in Ireland. There's only so much you can take in a big city like London, so when the opportunity came up to work in Ireland on a good part and a wonderful script, I jumped at it.'

It was a strange coincidence that she found herself playing another landlady but says,

'Phoebe and Assumpta couldn't be more different people, besides the different accents. Phoebe has been very good to me but actually it was nice to get out of these 1940s corsets and clothes. They can be a bit restricting!'

She says she isn't so outspoken as Assumpta but wishes that she had her confidence. Having said that, she has found that fans never say anything out of order to her, perhaps because Assumpta is such a fierce character.

Much has been written about the off-screen romance between Stephen and Dervla but they prefer to keep as low a public profile as possible and Dervla is keen to point out, 'Our relationship is important but we don't bring it to work with us.'

When their real life partnership hit the headlines, they tried to handle it in the best way they could. 'We certainly weren't going to deny going out with each other, but how do you balance it all?' she wondered.

In the end, the couple decided that they would beat the tabloids at their own game by admitting their relationship live on the Friday

Ballykissangel's annual Charity Slave Auction where folk bid for the right to three hours of someone's time – all in a good cause. Father Clifford finds himself working behind the bar.

night Northern Ireland show *PK Tonight,* followed by an appearance on *The Gaby Roslin Show.*

'It was a way of saying, "We have nothing to hide, we're quite normal, now forget about it,"' adds Dervla. 'But what's the problem, anyway? We're just two individuals, two actors, who happen to be going out together.'

Laughs Stephen, 'If you believe everything you read in the papers, we've been married, divorced, bought about three houses and had children – all of which has been news to us! The rest of the cast and the crew pin up whatever front page or centre spread about us they come across, and laugh themselves stupid about it, but that's as far as it goes. No-one's attitude changed in the slightest.' In the new series, Asumpta's final scenes mean there isn't a dry eye in the house and Stephen confesses his tears were for real.

Ballykissangel's real life location is the tiny village of Avoca in the south-eastern County Wicklow known as the Garden of Ireland, yet only sixty minutes' drive from Dublin. As the day trippers pour in to have their photographs

Scene from the top of Avoca village
(GEORGE HORNER)

Glendalough, the valley of two lakes, a monastic settlement dating from the sixth century and one of the jewels of Wicklow
(GEORGE HORNER)

taken and to enjoy a pint in The Fountain Bar which is the fictional Fitzgerald's, the pub where Assumpta presides behind the bar, they are quick to appreciate why Avoca was chosen as the setting for the series.

In the words of Thomas Moore on Avoca's *Meeting of the Waters*:

> *There is not in this wide world a valley so sweet*
> *As the vale in whose bloom these bright waters meet*
> *Oh, the last ray of feeling and hope must depart*
> *Ere the bloom of that valley shall fade from my heart.*

Natural beauty there may be in abundance but there is no doubt the series has brought a much needed economic contribution to the community. The village had been in serious decline since a nearby mine closed some fifteen years previously with the loss of 1,000 jobs. Unemployment problems in the valley meant that prior to the series, the economy was mainly

Brian Quigley (Tony Doyle), Assumpta (Dervla Kirwan), Father Peter Clifford (Stephen Tompkinson) and Niamh (Tina Kellegher)

reliant on tourism. That has been given a boost to the extent that as many as twenty coachloads a day passed through the tiny village as filming was in progress but Stephen says, 'They were all very good about letting us get on with it. Mind you, writer's cramp was setting in after a while because of all the autographs I was asked for, and I think the show should be sponsored by Kodak given the amount of snaps people were taking!'

The village has used money from the BBC to renovate the centre of their village and a couple of derelict buildings have been demolished to make way for a park.

Peter Moore, chairman of the Vale of Avoca Development Association points out that not only has the series encouraged people to visit the area but has given employment to a large number of Irish actors and other people involved in the film-making business.

Tony Doyle can perhaps sum up some of the

reasons for the enormous success of *Ballykissangel* : 'There's just a very special atmosphere here, which is caring and embracing but also gives you space to actually do the work. There isn't that sense of colossal pressure that you might get in London, though, up until fairly recently, Ireland didn't really get the benefit of major investment in film and television.

'Of course, *Ballykissangel* is a big project, but because it's filmed here there's still that special atmosphere which eases the pain of all the fourteen or fifteen hour days. The work gets done but everybody still enjoys each other's company.

'We're a bit like a very large, extended family, and hopefully, a lot of that special atmosphere, that quality, translates itself on to the screen.'

Producer Joy Lale knew that if the programme became a stereotyped parody of the Irish it would be doomed. Instead, as script editor she liaised with writer Keiran Prendiville at the outset and the resulting balance was the right formula to capture the public imagination.

Sadly, Joy was killed in a car crash on a country

Church and round tower at Glendalough (GEORGE HORNER)

road while returning from filming one night. Although the tragedy cast an enormous cloud over the cast and crew, Stephen explains, 'We all felt we had to finish it for Joy's sake, to do justice to all the work she had put into it. Everyone was devastated because we'd had a party for about six hundred people in the village just a couple of days before. After Joy's death, we all went down to hold Mass in Avoca and the place was absolutely heaving with people.'

Although the scripts do contain humour, they're far from frivolous. Says Tony, 'It seems that people are somehow bewitched and enchanted by the idea of this mythical village and these wonderful characters, but it's not all warmth and humour.

'*Ballykissangel* has the odd trauma and tragedy, too. It doesn't avoid the more serious issues that hit you in the face from time to time, and most episodes chew over one serious subject or another.'

The scripts must be pretty convincing as Stephen's fan mail includes plenty of encouragement from priests, not only Roman Catholic ones, who say they feel the programme's portrayals are convincing, concerning the struggles the clergy can have with their faith.

'They say it's very believable, and their basic message seems to be "Keep up the good work" which I think is fantastic,' says Stephen. 'Praise indeed!'

Stephen feels that one of the things people seem to like about Peter is that he doesn't pretend to have all the right answers. 'He never has an ideal solution, but hopefully he can offer a few more options than the traditional point of view within the Church allows, and encourage people to think more for themselves.'

A former altar boy until the age of seventeen, Stephen still attends Mass. He laughs as he says of his character, 'He's a bit much for me to live up to sometimes.'

He admits he had never been to Ireland before the first series of *Ballykissangel* was filmed. 'I've fallen in love with place and the people,' he reveals. 'He's a character I'd be happy to play again.'

What of plans for future series? We must await developments but there is one intriguing suggestion...

'One day this bunch of Oasis fans outside the Westbury Hotel in Dublin clocked me and said "Oh Jaysus, it's Priestman",' recalls Stephen. 'We're thinking about a spin-off series featuring a new superhero partnership – Priestman and Altarboy Wonder!'

6

ALL CREATURES GREAT AND SMALL

A whole host of TV programmes featuring animals have emerged in recent years. Fly-on-the wall documentaries of real life vets and animal hospitals are consistently high in the ratings lists, attracting huge audiences but the forerunner of them all was *All Creatures Great and Small*, inspired by the novels of James Herriot.

Between 1978 and 1989, the BBC showed 87 episodes and two Christmas specials, exporting the series to 42 countries and making James Herriot the most famous vet in the world. At its peak, the series attracted 20 million viewers.

Although he initially tried to keep it a closely guarded secret, the story was soon out that Herriot was the pen name of Alf

Wight. Although he spent nearly all of his adult life in Yorkshire, Alf Wight was not a Yorkshireman but was in fact born in Sunderland and brought up in Glasgow. After

Herriot Country – Langthwaite
(RICHMONDSHIRE DISTRICT COUNCIL)

James, Siegfried and an assortment of dogs, doing the rounds

graduating from veterinary college in 1939, he was offered a job with two Yorkshire vets, the Sinclair brothers, who became better known to viewers as Siegfried and Tristan Farnon . It wasn't until 1966 that 'James Herriot' decided to turn his hand to writing and after a few unsuccessful attempts to have his short stories published, turned instead to novels. His first book, *If Only They Could Talk* was published in 1970.

That first book was followed in 1972 by *It Shouldn't Happen to a Vet*. 1973 saw the publication of *Let Sleeping Vets Lie*, then *Vet in Harness in 1976, Vet in a Spin* in 1977 and *The Lord God Made Them All* in 1981. Three omnibus volumes were also released – *All*

Creatures Great and Small, *All Things Bright and Beautiful* and *All Things Wise and Wonderful*. James Herriot had become a best selling author.

Before the TV series began, two films were made for the cinema screen. *All Creatures Great and Small* in 1974 was the first with Simon Ward playing James Herriot, Lisa Harrow as Helen, Siegfried played by Anthony Hopkins and Brian Sterner as Tristan. There were some cast changes for the 1976 film *It Shouldn't Happen to a Vet* with John Alderton in the part of Herriot and Siegfried played by Colin Blakely.

It was producer Bill Sellars, browsing on a railway bookstall who first realised the potential to turn the best-selling books into a TV series.

A country boy, born and bred in Shropshire, Christopher Timothy was just about to complete filming a BBC comedy series and uncertain of his next career move when he heard rumours that he was being considered for the part of Herriot. He recalls in his own book *Vet Behind the Ears* that when he was summoned by

Swaledale near Reeth
(RICHMONDSHIRE DISTRICT
COUNCIL)

Christopher Timothy who delighted the 'real' James Herriot with his portrayal of the young country vet

Bill Sellars he was surprised to be offered the part of Tristan. He heard himself saying with what he describes as appalling clarity: 'I'm only interested in playing James Herriot'. He wondered afterwards whether he would live to regret that statement. It wasn't until ten long days later when he arrived home from a hard day's filming that he was finally told the part was his – by his fourteen-year-old son Simon. To say he was pleased would be to underestimate his reaction...

Christopher turned out to be perfect for the part and delighted Alf Wight with his portrayal of the young country vet. It was a role which taught him at least one thing – to have a healthier respect for animals. 'When you arrive at a location and see them for the first time it's always a daunting experience. They always appear much bigger than you expect!'

In 1980, he talked about his worst moment of the series they were currently filming. 'I had to examine a jet black stallion. It was absolutely huge and the fact that it was in a cramped stall meant I didn't have much room in which to move.'

The horse had been encouraged to be frisky for the scene but Christopher recalled, 'It was a bit too real for me! Hooves were flying everywhere – I couldn't get out fast enough! James Herriot's natural reaction in the real situation was one of terror, too, so no acting skill on my part was necessary – I was petrified anyway!'

The series wasn't all good, clean fun... 'I seem to spend most of my time up to my wellies in muck,' laughed Chris, 'but it makes you appreciate what country vets have to put up

Wensleydale sheep graze in the Dales countryside
(RICHMONDSHIRE DISTRICT COUNCIL)

Robert Hardy, as the
ebullient Siegfried

Bolton Castle
(RICHMONDSHIRE DISTRICT
COUNCIL)

with every day.'

Robert Hardy was chosen to play the ebullient Siegfried. In *If Only They Could Talk* Herriot described his first meeting with Siegfried, having assumed from his name that he would be a little, fat German vet. 'He was just about the most English man I had ever seen. Long, humorous, strong-jawed face. Small, clipped moustache, untidy, sandy hair. He was wearing an old tweed jacket and shapeless flannel trousers. The collar of his check shirt was frayed and the tie carelessly knotted. He looked as though he didn't spend much time in front of a mirror.'

Although Robert Hardy sported no moustache and his huntin', shootin', fishin' Siegfried was perhaps more tweedy rather than dishevelled, it was a fine piece of casting, with Siegfried bulldozing everyone with his boundless energy and enthusiasm. A keen horseman in real life, Robert offered the

Tristan, played by Peter
Davison, whose tangled
love life was apt to test
his brother's patience

'Milking time' – Wensley (RICHMONDSHIRE DISTRICT COUNCIL)

advice to Christopher Timothy 'Stay wary and you stay alive.'

At first, Robert had a few misgivings about the series. 'I said, "For goodness sake how are you going to do it?" because one could see it turning into *Vets at Large* and I didn't want that.'

But it soon became obvious that the series was a winner and Robert was obviously comfortable in the part. 'It's pretty marvellous to be in something you enjoy doing and find other people enjoy watching.'

It was just after the series was first screened that Robert received a facetious letter from his own vet. 'Just thought I'd ask you,' it read, 'if you'd be available for locum work, weekends only.'

Robert replied that he would be only too willing but that his price had gone up...

The part of Tristan was taken by Peter Davison, often the hapless victim of one of Siegfried's explosive rages which were enough to make the Skeldale House dogs run for cover.

Tristan's tendency to find himself in awkward

James, Helen (Lynda Bellingham) and family

scrapes was a constant source of irritation to his elder brother. More often then not, Tristan's tangled love life was the source of the problem.

'I'm no sex symbol,' insisted Peter. 'I just happen to be playing a good part! Tristan has quite an appealing image really.'

Actress Deborah Arnold remembers one scene when she was playing one of Tristan's girlfriends. They were filming a supposedly romantic scene high on the North York Moors in the depths of winter. 'When we kissed, it was so cold, our lips stuck together!' she laughs.

Peter Davison agrees that the weather could often be a little bracing.

'For some scenes in the last series I had to go up to a lamp before I said my lines because my mouth was so cold, I thought I couldn't speak. I'd stick my fingers in coffee to make them come to life.'

Carol Drinkwater was the first to play James's

wife Helen, followed by Lynda Bellingham in later episodes. Carol remembered filming in a very cold byre. 'Some of the cows were becoming rather excited and suddenly one of them showed it was no respector of actresses. It lifted its tail and before I could move, I was drenched. My frock was soaked. It even went into my wellies! That was one of the most unpleasant days I've ever spent because the dress, in the style of the late 1930s, was the only one on location so I had to continue wearing it for the rest of the sequence – and there were no other wellies my size...'

Some members of the cast weren't always so accommodating when things didn't go according to plan – the animals which were really the focus of the whole plot.

Ex-policeman Toby Veall was charged with the responsibility of finding the right animals for the parts and making sure that they were on

Tristan and Siegfried perform some delicate surgery...

Callum, the young
Scottish vet played by
John McGlynn, joins the
veterinary team in 1988

set at the right time. 'It's all very well writing about a sow rooting away, snorting and then grabbing a shovel and running off with it. But it's almost impossible to get one to behave that way at the right time,' he lamented at the time. 'It's very hard to train an animal for a specific part. Really it's a matter of finding one as close as possible to script demands. When the call is for an animal with a specific ailment I contact vets who will know if there's something of that order available.'

Cows could pose problems, too. A milking cow couldn't be collected until after morning milking and then had to be returned in time for milking again in the evening. On set, she would have to be kept as stress free as possible or it would affect her milk yield.

Another animal researcher for the series, Laurence Burns, had a few problems with Fred, the cat. According to the script, Boris was a cat who had a fight with an Alsatian dog and, amazingly, emerged victorious. 'The problem was to find a cat who would spit and lash out but not actually hurt the actors,' he explained. It was then that a local vet remembered Fred, a cat who bit and scratched when he had to give it an injection.

The trouble was that Fred was a hunting cat and when Laurence went to collect him for his starring role he had disappeared on a rabbit hunt. 'I spent three-quarters of an hour trying to find the thing. Eventually his owner coaxed him into a cat box.' Even then, Fred was a reluctant performer and disappeared into a wood shed. In the end, Laurence had no choice but to find a replacement.

Director Peter Moffatt was keen to assure viewers that no animal was ever harmed during the making of the series. 'Everything is faked,' he said, 'or done by the techniques of television filming. No matter how realistic some things may look, we have never wounded or injured any animal.'

Animal breeds have changed since the 1930s when the series was set. At that time, Shorthorn cattle were very popular in the Yorkshire Dales whereas today Fresians have taken their place, so Shorthorns had to be specially recruited for the programme. Horses, too, had to be 'imported' from neighbouring counties. When a Charolais cow appeared in one episode, letters flooded in pointing out that the breed didn't arrive in Britain until well after World War 2.

In fact, any anachronisms were always spotted by eagle-eyed viewers. Said the props man despairingly, 'The trouble is so many people have got freeze-frame videos these days they can sit at home and study every frame in minute detail. We make one mistake and they are on us. It's a nightmare.'

The series had two practising vets acting as advisors, giving hints and tips to the actors so that the presentation was as authentic as possible. When tricky 'operations' had to be performed, the skin of a dead animal would be placed over the live beast so that the 'vet' could be seen cutting into the skin.

Animal star of the show, the notorious Pekinese, Tricki-Woo, was discovered when he visited one of the real vets' surgeries. The pampered pet of Mrs Pumphrey (Margaretta Scott), soon attracted fan mail by the sackload. 'At first we wondered what to do with them,' said a spokesman for the BBC. 'When we opened them we found they were chatty letters asking for an autograph and signed with a name like "Sammy Spaniel" or "Tiger the Terrier". So we answered the fan mail enclosing a picture when asked for.'

Tricky-Woo Mark 11 was played by a six-year-old bitch ('The sex doesn't matter; no one can tell under all that hair') discovered and chaperoned by Jessie Round, a pet broker and doggie chaperone for the film industry. The original Tricki-Woo's untimely demise had caused a major panic search for a substitute.

According to the English Tourist Board at the time, *All Creatures Great and Small* did for North Yorkshire what Thomas Hardy did for Dorset. The 20 mile radius surrounding Richmond quickly became known as Herriot country.

'Skeldale House' surgery was located in the fictional Darrowby in the Yorkshire Dales whereas the real veterinary practice where Alf Wight was based was at Thirsk, with a partner practice at Leyburn. Half way between the market town of Hawes and Scarborough, Thirsk does not lie in the Yorkshire Dales but the vets' work would take them all over the area. The real Leyburn partner, Frank Bingham, was Herriot's inspiration for the character of Ewan Ross.

Herriot's first impression of the dales is recounted in his book *If Only They Could Talk*. 'Darrowby didn't get much space in the guide books but when it was mentioned it was described as a grey little town on the river Darrow with a cobbled market place and little

of interest except its two ancient bridges. But when you looked at it, its setting was beautiful on the pebbly river where the houses clustered thickly and straggled unevenly along the lower slopes of Herne Fell. Everywhere in Darrowby, in the streets, through the windows of the houses you could see the Fell rearing its calm, green bulk more than two thousand feet above the huddled roofs.'

In actual fact, Darrowby was a mixture of Thirsk, Richmond, Middleham and Leyburn with a bit of imagination thrown in. The film crew settled on the Dales village of Askrigg for the location of Darrowby. A stone house fronted by wrought iron railings on the main street was used as Skeldale House. Tourists would clamour to be photographed outside with their pet dogs as thought they were waiting for a consultation. The village shop during filming would replace its window display with 1930s goods. The Kings Arms, a former coaching inn, doubled as The Drovers Arms for the series.

Most of the local people appreciated the boost to the local economy and although the village is still recognised as one of the most famous landmarks of 'Herriot Country', with the cameras, cast and crew of *All Creatures Great and Small* long since departed, life has returned to a less hectic pace.

7
LAST OF THE SUMMER WINE

In June 1997, BBC's *Last of the Summer Wine* celebrated its 25th year of production, making it a record-breaker as the longest running sitcom in the world, still enjoying viewing figures of over 8 million.

Creator of the programme, Roy Clarke, has mapped out the antics of Compo, Clegg, Foggy and friends since 1972 when Holmfirth in West Yorkshire was chosen to make a pilot programme for the Comedy Playhouse series.

Duncan Wood, head of BBC comedy in 1972 remembers, 'I was sitting at home one evening watching a series called *The Misfits*. Here was a show which was supposed to be a drama but with comedy undertones. I thought the phrasing and the writing and the whole style of it was very much worthwhile pursuing. The writer was a guy I'd never met called Roy Clarke.'

Nora Batty's
(KIRKLEES TOURISM)

Foggy (Brian Wilde), Compo (Bill Owen) and Clegg (Peter Sallis) – kids who happen to have got a bit older.

Roy Clarke takes up the story: 'Duncan Wood invited me to go and see him and asked would I be interested in having a crack at sitcom. They had a requirement for a comedy series based around three old men.

'For a long time I struggled with this idea to try and get some enthusiasm about it but I had none at all really – until, at the point of almost turning it down, it occurred to me that if three old men were totally free and had no responsibilities or ties and they each lived alone, they were unmarried or widowed, they were unem-ployed or retired therefore they were able to wander about in the same way as young adolescents and that's what pulled it out of the fire – the fact that I saw them not so much as old people but just as kids who happen to have got a bit older...

'The characters came fairly easily with Compo coming first because Compo was a composite of people I knew in my own environment and my own area who lived that totally feckless but quite cheerful existence – and always wore wellies! Having got him, it made

Ivy (Jane Freeman), Nora
(Kathy Staff) and Edie
(Dame Thora Hird)

Holmfirth – the location
suggested by Barry Took
(KIRKLEES TOURISM)

obvious sense to go straight to his opposite who was regimented, straight up and down, authoritarian so you got the two extremes which left a nice slot for Clegg in the middle who would sort of take the blows and balance things out.'

Then it was a question of looking for the right actors to fill the roles.

'I wanted Peter Sallis from the word one if he was available. I'd written it very much with Peter in mind. The other two I had no fixed ideas about and left it with Jimmy Gilbert.'

James Gilbert hadn't seen Peter Sallis since they we were at RADA together about twenty years previously. His first impression when he saw Peter coming in wearing a rather battered jacket, a cardigan and ill-fitting trousers was 'He's a bit down on his luck' but as Peter was leaving, he turned and he said, 'I think this would do for Clegg, don't you?'

Smiles Peter, who is also the voice of Wallace in the award winning animated films of *Wallace and Gromit* by Nick Park, 'It was a suit I'd had for many years and which I thought would make rather a good suit for Clegg, a sort of a library lounger's suit. What of course I didn't realise was that the series was going to last for more than twenty years. And it was about twenty years later that it was decided it had so many holes in it, it would have to be rebuilt! They went to the local mill, gave them a bit of the cloth and lo and behold they produced a whole roll and made me a completely new suit.'

James Gilbert remembers his thoughts on casting the character of Compo. 'I thought that

Bill Owen would be right because I'd seen him play a very Compo-like character in a play with Spike Milligan and I'd also seen him in another play where he was playing a real tough northerner. Putting the two together and having seen him in comedy and working in a musical, he seemed to be the perfect casting.'

Roy Clarke was unconvinced, having previously associated Bill's work with films where he would be playing roles such as a Cockney airman. 'I couldn't see Bill as Compo. I wasn't until we had a read through that I began to see

Nora gives Compo a telling off - again!

Summer Wine Country
(KIRKLEES TOURISM)

that Bill could play Compo and as soon as he was on screen the rest of the world could see that he could play Compo!'

Bill remembers reading the script in bed. 'I got about half way through and rang Jimmy Gilbert, the director and producer. "What do you think?" he said. I said, "It's pure gold. Count me in!"'

The third member of the trio was Michael Bates who took the part of Blamire. Then it was a question of finding a location. Roy Clarke had originally thought of Rotherham with the

action taking place in an urban set-up but the director felt it should be a small market town surrounded by beautiful countryside preferably with valleys.

It was TV presenter Barry Took who suggested they try Holmfirth as it sounded exactly what they were looking for. 'I rang up Roy,' he says, 'and we went to Holmfirth and stood on top of the hill looking down at the town and we both said "That's it!"'

Last of the Summer Wine was something of a breakthrough in visual terms as a situation comedy which wasn't studio bound. The scenery was relevant to the plots and from the beginning has been a major element in its success.

Peter Sallis remembers setting off from Shepherd's Bush in June 1972 with Jimmy Gilbert, Bill Owen and Michael Bates and finding themselves in little country pub on Saddleworth Moor. None of them could then have envisaged that the series was going to be such an unprecedented success.

Says Peter, 'Sometimes you're lucky in an actor's life and something special turns up. When I read *Last of the Summer Wine* I thought this was it.'

The BBC originally disliked the title – '*Last of the Summer Wine*? – not a comedy title!' And they weren't keen on the music either at the outset. 'A string quartet? Not the sort of music associated with situation comedies.' Who would have expected a beautiful melody like Ronnie Hazelhurst penned for the programme? The theme tune has since been adapted as a march, a quickstep, even in the style of Dallas.

Roy Clarke explains, 'Because the story was going to be about old people I wanted to

Another of the trio's adventures which is destined not to go according to plan...

Holmfirth, where tourism
has boomed since the
programme began
(KIRKLEES TOURISM)

Nora Batty and husband

emphasise that summer was still around. It might be the last of summer but it was still summer as far as these guys were concerned so that's why I called it *Last of the Summer Wine* to emphasise the summer as against the autumn. It (the title) was never well received, it was always taken for granted that I'd have to change this and keep it for a while as a working title until we found a better one. One of the alternatives was *The Library Mob* because in the first series, they regularly used to visit their library and sit in the reading room, leafing through the news-papers and chatting. Fortunately it was aban-doned just before the show went out on air and we reverted to *Last of the Summer Wine*.'

James Gilbert recalls, 'After we'd done the pilot, a deputation of three actors came along to see me and said "We don't think this is going to work as *Last of the Summer Wine*. Nobody will remember it". Now, 25 years later, it's still there.'

The location of Holmfirth did turn out to be perfect. Barry Took says, 'Well, you can see why I suggested Holmfirth. It has practically everything. I had made a documentary here some months before that and I had found the town absolutely charming, peaceful and utterly delightful.

'I called my 1971 film *Having a Lovely Time*, an oblique reference to Bamforths (a local firm) who published seaside postcards and surprisingly had a successful movie business making comedy films at Holmfirth some sixty years before *Last of the Summer Wine*.

'I ended my film by speculating that in twenty years' time, Holmfirth would probably be exactly the same. How wrong can you be? Nowadays, tourism has taken over ...'

'Holmfirth has always been on my conscience to some extent,' confesses Roy Clarke, because it's been such a spectacular find. It's always been so beautiful on the screen and I've always had a very warm spot for that area since I first saw it. And I've also always had a rather guilty feeling about what we've done to the place.'

But no-one can deny that it has brought business to the area.

Reservoir, near Holmfirth – showing the characteristic drystone walls of *Summer Wine Country* (KIRKLEES TOURISM)

Ivy's cafe really is a cafe where you can buy Ivy's delicious scones topped with jam and fresh dairy cream but whatever you do, warns a notice, do not park cycles in front of the window! Until the BBC left its set there, following filming of *Getting Sam Home* in 1983, the cafe was a paint store for the adjacent ironmongers and had to be converted for the filming of each series. The inside of the cafe as well as all the sets in the series have been made in the film studios at Shepperton.

Wesley's Garage – now a feature of the series – was a hurried last-minute 'find' when the original choice of location was suddenly surrounded by bulldozers preparing a new housing development. Auntie Wainwright's shop is a studio-made set. When the crew originally filmed it, it was a lovely old shop but when they came back a year later it was a private house so the designer had to build a facade of a shop and bolt it to the front of the house. Compo's house (below Nora Batty's) was only a cellar, but now houses the *Last of The Summer Wine* exhibition which Bill Owen was asked to design.

Eastergate Bridge, Marsden
(KIRKLEES TOURISM)

'I tried to explain through photographs and information and some memories a vague impression of the history of this remarkable little television series. The other part of the exhibition is set up as Compo's living room. Of course the pearl of the exhibition, certainly in that room, are my long johns which hang in front of the fire. I've heard that ladies have swooned as they've looked at them.'

Bob Eltringham, the cast's dresser, adds,

The terrible trio

'It's all very well Bill putting his underwear in the exhibition but I dress him and sometimes I've got to go and raid that exhibition to get them back!'

Holmfirth's increasing fame has brought its own difficulties. At one time, Sunday was the best day for filming – quiet with very little traffic but the influx of *Summer Wine* sightseers has meant that Sunday is now the busiest day of the week in the village and filming has to take place elsewhere.

Nora Batty's terrace house is privately owned by Sonia Whitehead who says, 'The BBC have been filming at my house for 25 years, twice a year without fail. I'm getting used to it. They change my doors and take all my flowers away, everything. I'm getting used to the tourists as well but if they want to see anything funny, it won't be at my house, it'll be on the television!'

When filming takes place, Nora Batty's blue door takes the place of Sonia's own, the satellite dish is taken down and various shop signs removed, ready for Nora, the object of Compo's unrequited lust, to take her place as monarch of all she surveys at the top of the steps, her trusty broom at hand.

'A lot of people think there wasn't life before Nora Batty,' says Kathy Staff, who isn't a Yorkshirewoman but comes from Cheshire, 'but actually I did ten parts in *Coronation Street,* I did four series of *Sez Les* with Les Dawson and I also did seven years in *Crossroads* playing Doris Luke. It was then that Terry Wogan took an interest. He announced one day that he thought that Doris Luke was Nora Batty's sister and from then on he decided that he would be secretary of the Nora Batty fan club. He actually gave me a midnight blue suspender belt with a little pink rose right in the centre.'

There is little chance for Kathy to appear glamorous as Nora – as well as having to wear unflattering padding to augment her figure, hair curlers and the famous wrinkled stockings are her usual accessories. But far from being the formidable character she appears on screen, Kathy is warm and approachable and devotes her free time to her family, her religious activities – her younger daughter is a curate – and to community organisations.

Bill Owen remembers one particularly hairy moment when the trio were being filmed in a car with a camera mounted on the bonnet and the car ended up in the duck pond . 'The car began to sink, the water was coming in all through the doors and a voice was heard from the director "Save the camera!" I replied – but I can't tell you what I said – the BBC don't allow it! Even then when we got on the shore the director said "That was wonderful, we'll do it again as a long shot". He turned to us. We weren't there, we were in our caravan. He did get the shot – but not with us!'

It was when Michael Bates sadly died in 1976 that Brian Wilde was brought in to play a slightly modified Blamire character, Foggy Dewhurst. When Foggy departed for pastures new in 1984, Michael Aldridge took his place as Professor Seymour Utterthwaite, leaving in 1990 when viewers then saw the return of Foggy.

Seymour's sister Edie was played by Dame Thora Hird. Although it was a guest appearance, she has been with the cast ever since! 'I'm a new girl in this company,' laughs Thora. 'I've only been with them thirteen years. The funny thing about the programme is that it's about simple things. The things people laugh at are the things they do themselves.'

For instance, she remembers her own mother setting great store by checking that the house was secured locked up before they left home. Despite the fact that it was like Fort Knox they had 'nowt worth pinching'.

Celebrity guests often make an appearance. Jean Alexander of Hilda Ogden fame was another character who appeared originally for a couple of Christmas specials and was asked to join the ranks on a permanent basis as Auntie Wainwright and even John Cleese made a guest appearance in the 1993 Christmas episode.

'It's always very pleasurable to have guests like Ron Moody,' says Roy Clarke. 'I saw his wonderful performance in *Oliver* as Fagin. It's always the completion of a dream when someone like Ron Moody appears in a major part, even if it's only in one episode.'

Last of the Summer Wine is the only situation comedy which is all film and made for Widescreen. Every episode is shown to a live invited audience and their laughter is recorded.

'I wouldn't want canned laughter that wasn't genuine,' says Roy Clarke, 'but I wouldn't want no laughter at all.'

Sometimes, the audience reaction is even more enthusiastic than the team expected. Says Bill Owen, 'We sometimes leave a gap at the end of a line when a laugh is indicated but sometimes that laugh lasts longer than we anticipated and it has to be taken out.'

The *Last of the Summer Wine* Appreciation Society was formed quite late in the day in its 21st year and enjoys a worldwide following from all age groups. Even the Queen is said to be a fan, rumoured to have rung the BBC once on return from a Royal tour, to request an update on the antics of her favourite characters.

So, what of the future? Says Roy Clarke, 'If the series begins to slide then it wants burying with great pomp and ceremony but if the audience is still out there and fond of it I'd love to do another one.'

83-year-old Bill Owen has the last word. 'My problem is, what am I going to do when it finishes?'